William Bolcom

Little Suite of Four Dances

For E♭ Clarinet and Piano

(1984)

I.   Rag
II. Apache-Jungle
III. Quasi-Waltz (*Hommage* to Joseph Kosma)
IV. Soft Shoe

*Commissioned by and dedicated to Conrad Josias
in memory of his father, Murray Josias*

Duration: *ca.* 6'30"

ISBN 978-0-634-05545-4

EDWARD B. MARKS MUSIC COMPANY / EXCLUSIVELY DISTRIBUTED BY HAL•LEONARD® CORPORATION

7777 W. BLUEMOUND RD. P.O. BOX 13819 MILWAUKEE, WI 53213

Commissioned by and dedicated to Conrad Josias – in memory of his father, Murray Josias

Little Suite of Four Dances E♭ Clarinet and Piano

I. Rag

By William Bolcom

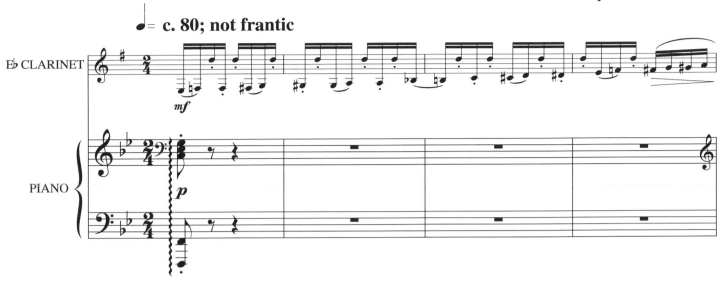

Carefree

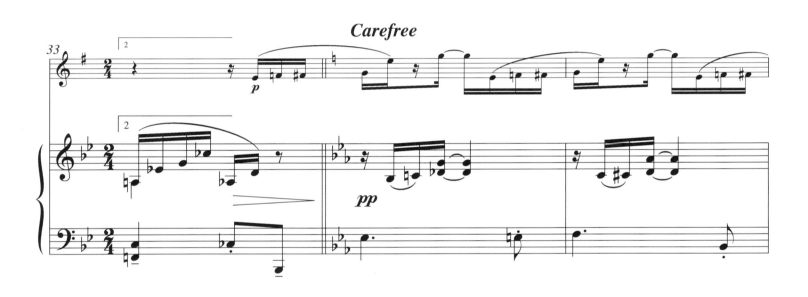

Nov. 25, 1984
Ann Arbor

II. Apache-Jungle

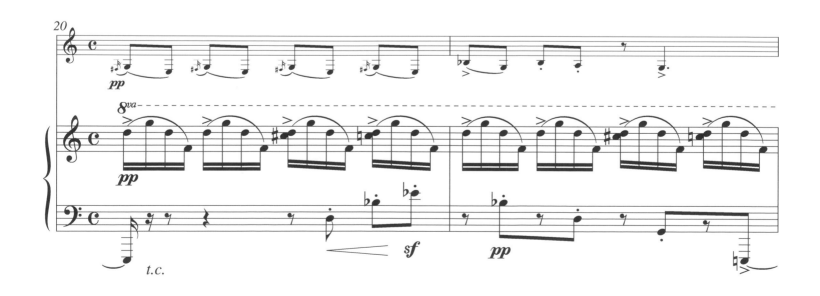

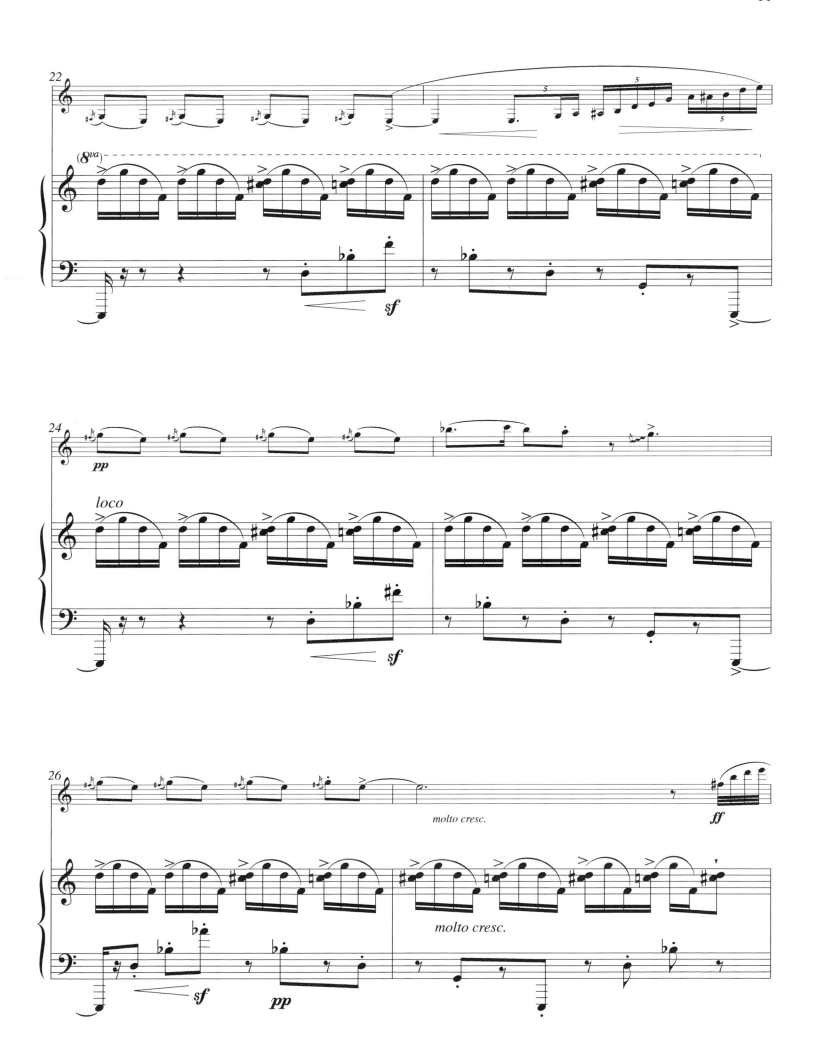

Commissioned by and dedicated to Conrad Josias – in memory of his father, Murray Josias

Little Suite of Four Dances
E♭ Clarinet and Piano

By William Bolcom

I. Rag

II. Apache-Jungle

Fast, aggressive ♩ = 126

III. Quasi-Waltz
Hommage to Joseph Kosma*

Simple and flowing (♩ = 100 ±)
poco rubato throughout

*Joseph Kosma was the composer of many songs with Jacques Prévert; the most famous is "Autumn Leaves."

THIS PAGE BLANK FOR TURNS

IV. Soft Shoe

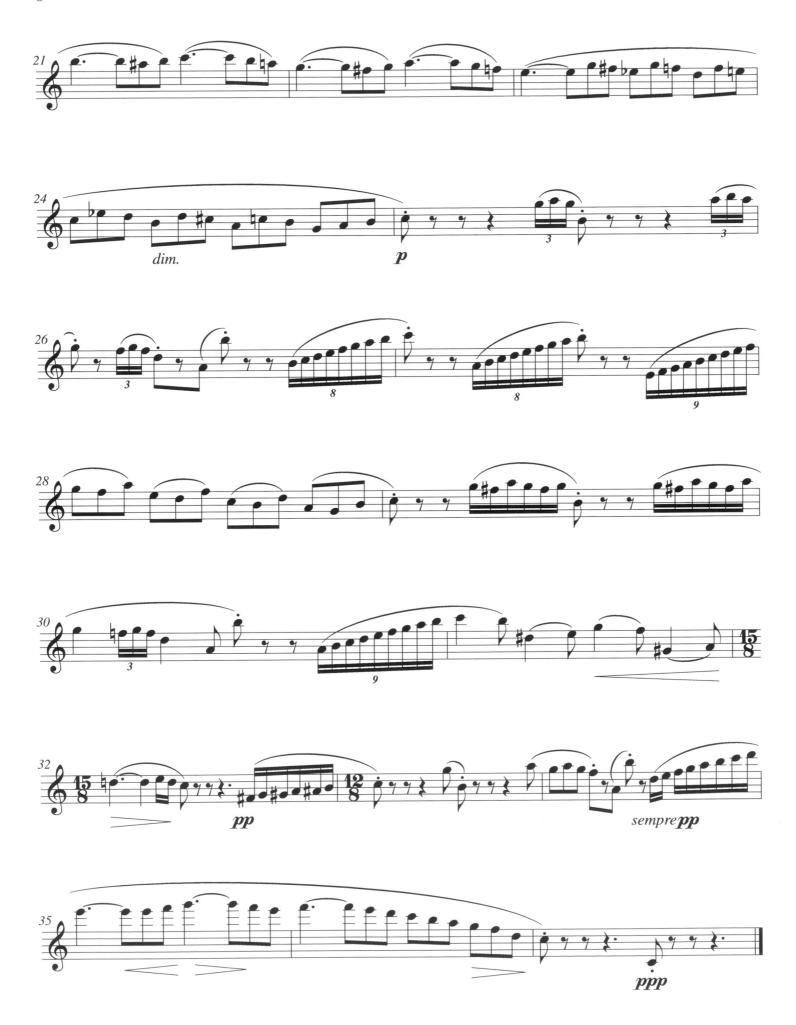

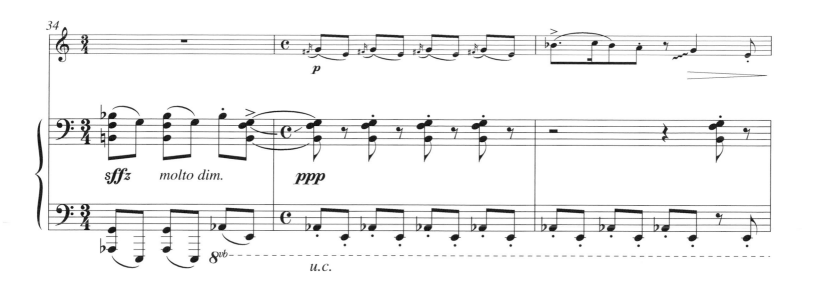

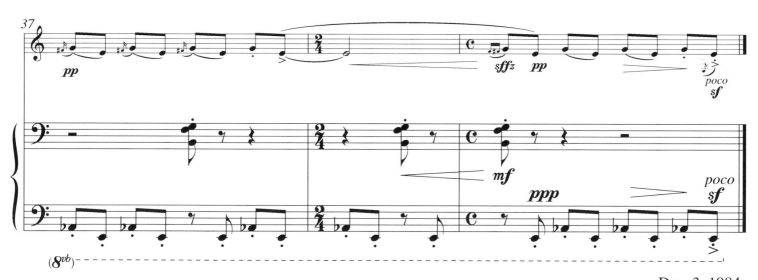

Dec. 3, 1984
Ann Arbor

III. Quasi-Waltz

Hommage to Joseph Kosma*

Simple and flowing (♩ =**100** ±)

poco rubato throughout

*Joseph Kosma was the composer of many songs with Jacques Prévert; the most famous is "Autumn Leaves."

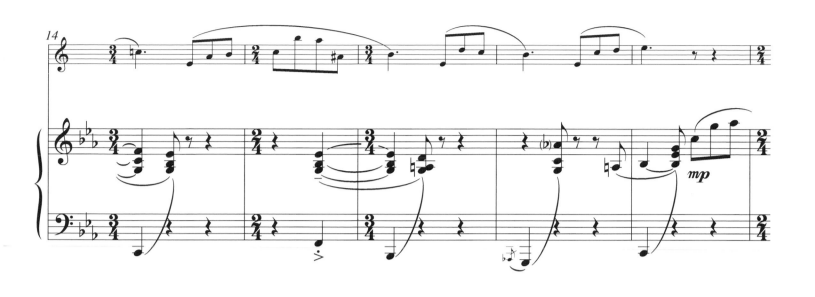

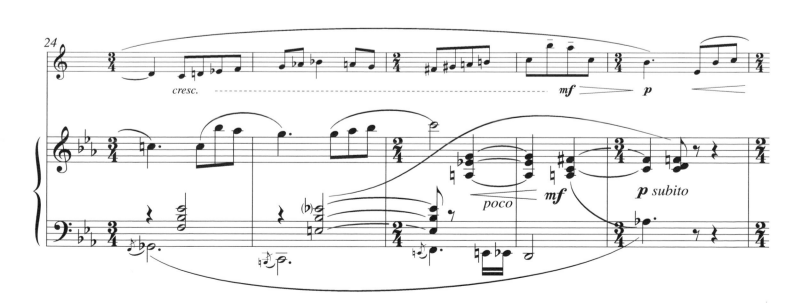

Nov. 28, 1984
Washington D.C.

IV. Soft Shoe

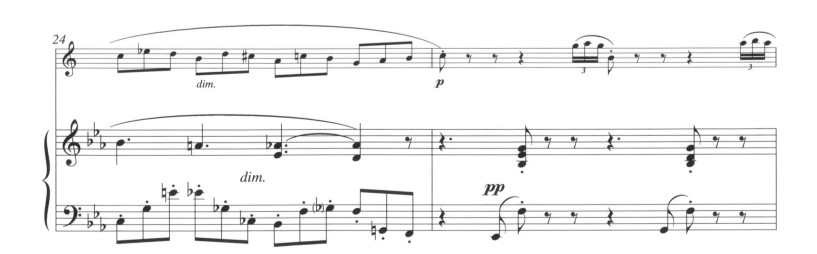

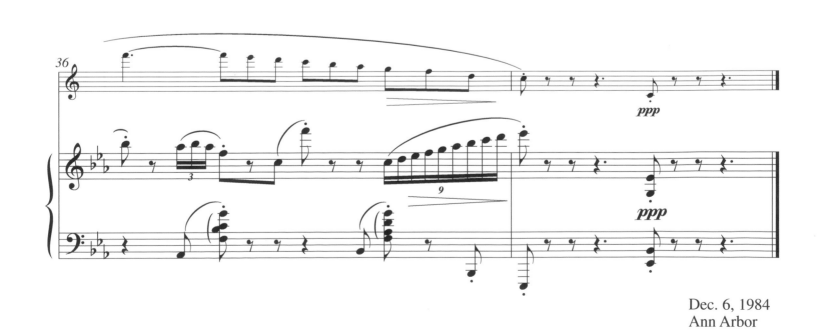

Dec. 6, 1984
Ann Arbor